Friendship
in *Action*

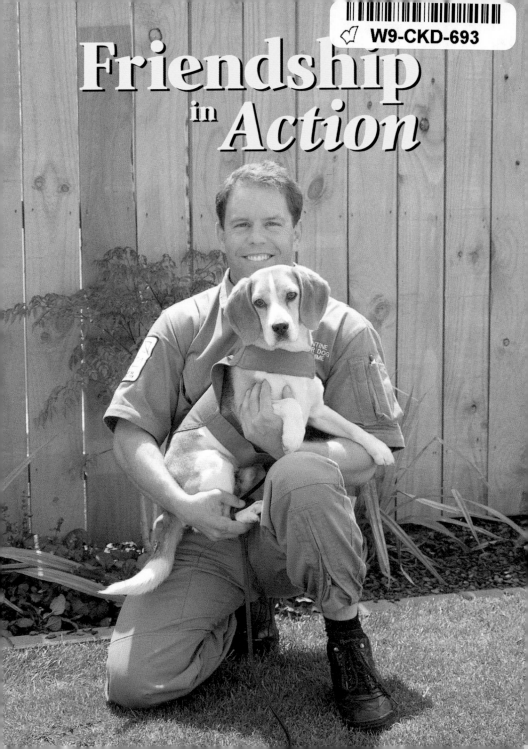

Contents

Sharing Our World

People and animals have shared the earth for a long time – perhaps for millions of years. In some cases, we have lived together well. In other cases, we have caused some animals to become **endangered** or **extinct**.

Over the years, people have formed strong friendships and working relationships with many groups of animals.

Dutiful Dogs

Dogs have lived and worked with people for more than 12,000 years. Gradually, as dogs have become **domesticated,** people have trained them to help with many tasks.

Some types of dogs are bred for certain abilities. The patient, friendly Labrador makes a very good guide dog. Huskies can cope very well in cold weather, and sheepdogs can quickly learn how to herd sheep.

The Beagle Brigade

Colvin Brannaka is an expert dog trainer. In just 12 weeks, he can train beagles to inspect luggage for foods that are not allowed to come into a country.

Beagles are ideal for this work because they have an excellent sense of smell and a quiet, friendly nature. They work very well with people and can inspect luggage without upsetting the traveler.

The beagles Colvin works with are so well trained, they can sniff out the difference between food that is harmful and food that is safe. They can sniff out oranges that could carry pests, but will ignore orange juice that does not.

Left: Dog handler, Rene Gloor, and Benny, the beagle

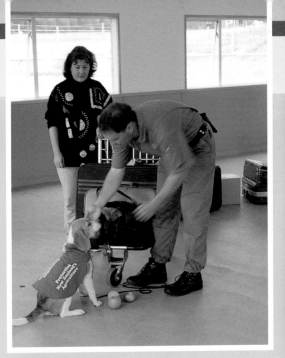

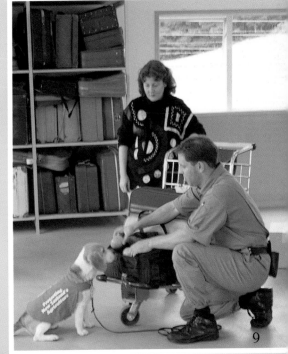

9

The Beagle Training School

In an interview, Colvin Brannaka explained how he trains his beagles and the "detective teams" who handle them.

At what age are the puppies ready to start training?

I begin to train the puppies when they are 49 days old. At this age, they are ready to cope with learning.

Are all beagle puppies suitable for training?

No. Only about 40 percent have the qualities to learn really fast. I choose the right puppies by watching how they behave in a variety of new situations.

How do you manage to train them in just 12 weeks?

I choose the right learning activities, at the right learning pace, with the right rewards. The beagles learn to sniff out one food at a time so they don't get the 20 food scents mixed up.

Is it difficult to choose the right people to train as dog handlers?

Yes. The beagles and their handlers will have to work together for six years, so I choose people who are enthusiastic about doing this work for such a long period of time.

The Cat Shelter

One evening a week,
my mom and I do
volunteer work at the
local cat shelter.

The shelter has about 50 cats. Some cats
have their own cages. The rest are free to
roam around the shelter.

The first thing my mom and I do when we arrive is check a list to see how many cats are there. Cats are adopted quite often,  and sometimes I don't get a chance to say good-bye to them.

Then, we dish the food into a small bowl for each caged cat, and into large bowls for the roaming cats to share. Surprisingly, the cats are good at taking turns eating.

Next, we clean out the litter boxes. No one really likes to do this job.

When the cats have finished eating, we collect the dirty bowls and wash them. We recycle all the cat food cans.

Then comes the part I like the most. We pet and brush the cats. They love to be brushed and held, and I love to hold them, too!

I find it hard to leave the cats, because they usually want more attention. So, I turn on the radio for them to listen to before I leave.

Bird Rescue

Many people love birds and admire them for their beauty and song. However, there are many human activities that hurt birds. Sometimes, the river, stream, lagoon, or estuary homes of birds are polluted by people who live or work near them. Oil slicks from ships can also cause great harm.

Organizations, such as Bird Rescue, have been set up to help distressed or injured birds. Volunteers rescue birds that are tangled in fishing lines, have broken wings from hitting power lines, or are sick from disease.

Bird Rescue volunteers often become so well known that people bring them birds at any time of the day or night.

Pam to the Rescue

Twenty-five years ago, when Pam Howlett began her volunteer work, she knew very little about caring for sick, injured, and distressed birds.

But after years of experience and reading every book on birds she could find, she now finds that even veterinarians call her for help.

Injured birds are sent to Pam for long-term care. Last year, she cared for more than 2,000 sick and injured birds!

Like many volunteers, Pam spends her own money on food and medical supplies for her birds. In the future, she hopes more wildlife **rehabilitation** centers can be set up to take care of all the sick birds she is unable to help.

Saving Our Little Blues

Leila McNamara likes blue penguins so much that she has been saving them for the last 30 years. But Leila is also well known for saving gulls, ducks, doves, and pigeons, too.

Leila regularly watches the tides near her shoreline home.

Every day at high tide, she catches herring and mackerel for her hungry birds. Every day at low tide, she takes the penguins for a dip in some rock pools.

So far, more than 30 blue penguins have benefited from Leila's care. And her dedication and enthusiasm will certainly mean that more injured birds will be saved, too.

People like Pam and Leila and their volunteers spend many hours helping and caring for their bird friends.

The Gardener's Friend

Many people think of hedgehogs as pests that carry diseases. But hedgehogs can be very helpful, especially to gardeners, because they eat slugs and snails that can harm plants.

Hedgehogs are nocturnal animals, which means they are mainly active at night. Many nocturnal animals are endangered by living near people. Hedgehogs, possums, koalas, and badgers are often in danger of being hit by motorists, especially at night.

NEXT
8 km

Hedgehog Hospital

Marlene Barr and her son, Ari, are hedgehogs' friends. Marlene even set up her own hedgehog hospital. In an interview, she explains how it happened.

Where did you find your first sick hedgehog?

I found it eating our cat's food and knew that a hedgehog found during the day wasn't well. It looked very sick and it didn't have many **quills.**

What did you do?

After making sure the hedgehog had food, warmth, and shelter in our garden shed, I contacted some local animal centers.

They sent me to a veterinarian, who gave the hedgehog an injection for mange, which is a disease that causes the hedgehog's quills to fall out. I was told the hedgehog would need another injection in three weeks.

So how do you care for hedgehogs at your home?

We set up our garden shed with boxes, newspaper, hot-water bottles, eyedroppers, and water trays. And we make sure we have plenty of cat food and snails.

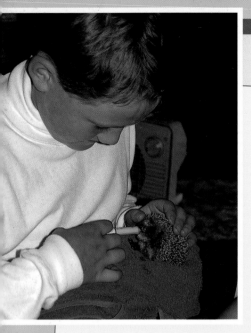

What duties does Ari have?

Ari keeps the pens clean, refills the water trays, and makes sure the hedgehogs have enough food. He also feeds the baby hedgehogs cat food and uses an eyedropper to feed them warm goat's milk.

How do you know when to release your "patients"?

The average stay in the hospital is about five weeks. A hedgehog is ready to be set free when it has enough quills to protect itself.

Where do you find sick hedgehogs?

People bring them to our house. But recently, a lone hedgehog arrived in a taxi. The carefully boxed-up hedgehog came with a note explaining why it was there.

Do other people help, too?

Yes. Friends help at the hospital if we are away. People leave bags of snails at the door, and veterinarians give us discounts.

Helping Hooves

For people who use wheelchairs, riding horses can be a very positive experience. Organizations, such as Riding for the Disabled Association (RDA), have volunteers who share their time and **equestrian** knowledge with people who are physically challenged.

Each rider has two "walkers" to guide and help control the horse. Walkers also teach the rider new skills and help them build their confidence and independence.

The horses are carefully chosen for their quiet nature and their willingness to follow instructions.

Most programs teach the rider to **groom,** saddle, lead, and feed a horse.

Getting on and off a horse safely is important, too. Special equipment, such as ramps and platforms, is often needed. Sometimes extra helpers are needed, too.

Some riders will always need the help of walkers, but others may learn to ride independently. Eventually, they may go on to become RDA volunteers themselves.

Glossary and Index

domesticated – tame animals that have learned to live with people

endangered – a species that is in danger of dying out

equestrian – anything to do with horseback riding

extinct – the complete dying out of a species

groom – to clean or brush

quills – the sharp spines of a hedgehog or porcupine

rehabilitation – training or guiding an animal back to health or independence

From the Author

The idea for this book came to me when I read an article about Marlene and Ari's Hedgehog Hospital. I showed the article to lots of people, who were as charmed by the story as I was. Then they started to tell me about other people who spend their lives caring for animals.

While I was writing this book, I did a lot of research. I had to set up interviews, find newspaper articles, and check facts with experts. But it was all worthwhile because I learned so much about animals from the people who care for them.

Erin Hanifin

A special thanks to Yvonne Morrison and James Gilberd for the story and photographs for the Cat Shelter.

Written by **Erin Hanifin**
Edited by **Anne-Marie Heffernan**
Designed by **Kristie Rogers**
Photographic research by **Sarah Irvine**

Photography by **James Gilberd:** (child with food for cats, cover; child stroking cat, cover and pp. 2-3; pp. 12-15); **Erin Hanifin:** (Ari with hedgehog, cover; pp. 24-25); **Sarah Irvine:** (trainer with beagle by baggage, cover; title page; pp. 8-11); **David Lowe:** (Rota with horse, cover; pp. 26-27); **Graham Meadows:** (p.6; dog herding sheep, p. 7; pp. 28-29); **N.Z. Herald:** (Pam with birds, p. 17; pp. 18-19; p. 23); **N.Z. Picture Library:** (p. 20); **Photobank:** (pp. 4-5; dog sledding, pp. 6-7; trash in water, p. 17; p. 21)

04 03 02 01 00
10 9 8 7 6 5 4

Distributed in the United States of America by
    Rigby
    a division of Reed Elsevier Inc.
    P.O. Box 797
    Crystal Lake, IL 60039-0797

Printed by Colorcraft, Hong Kong
ISBN: 0-7901-1646-4